Small Miracles

The Wonder of a Child

Paintings by
Sandra Kuck

Text by
Lisa Guest

HARVEST HOUSE PUBLISHERS

EUGENE, OREGON

Small Miracles

Paintings by Sandra Kuck
Text by Lisa Guest

Copyright © 1997 by Harvest House Publishers
Eugene, Oregon 97402

ISBN 0-7369-1104-9

Design and production by Garborg Design Works, Minneapolis, Minnesota

Harvest House Publishers has made every effort to trace the ownership of all quotes and poems in this book. In the event of any question from the use of any quote or poem, we regret any error made and will be pleased to make the necessary correction in future editions of this book.

"All You Are" by Michael Card, Copyright © 1989 Birdwing Music (ASCAP). Used by permission.

Scripture quotations are from the New American Standard Bible, © 1960, 1962, 1963, 1968, 1971, 1972, 1973, 1975, 1977 by The Lockman Foundation. Used by permission.

Printed in Hong Kong

03 04 05 06 07 08 09 /NG/ 7 6 5 4 3 2 1

All You Are

Where did you get those eyes so blue?
They're from the sky that you passed through
Where did you get that little tear?
Did you find that it was waiting for you here?

And what about your little nose?
He knew you'd need it for a rose
And as for your soft curly ear
He knew there would be songs for you to hear

For all you are, and all you'll be
For everything you mean to me
Though I don't understand
I know you're from the Father's hand

How can it be, that you are you?
He thought you up and so you grew
Because you're mine, it must be true
That He was also thinking of me too

Michael Card

My Little Miracle

How can I love so intensely someone I barely know?

Someone who has said not a word and shared not a thought,

someone who has yet to see a page of the calendar turn...

I wait for a glimmer of recognition in those shining eyes...

I look for a hint of a smile as I hold you close...

Through the night, I check your cradle, looking for the rising and

falling of your chest and straining to hear your soft breaths...

How can I love so intensely someone I barely know? I didn't know it was

possible—until there was you, my little miracle, my little mystery.

I will give thanks to Thee for I am fearfully and wonderfully made.

THE BOOK OF PSALMS

4

A Mother's Hopes

May you delight in the beauty and wonder of this big world

May you come to know what is right and what is wrong

May you smile often and laugh freely

May you be able to stand strong in what you believe

May you live life with energy and enthusiasm

May you have wisdom when it comes to choosing friends and activities

May you be aware of the precious gift of each day

Most of all, Little One, may you know that you are treasured and loved

I love these little people; and it is not a slight thing when they,
who are so fresh from God, love us.

CHARLES DICKENS

A Precious Gift

Good morning, my little one! And it is a good morning!

How could it be anything else as another day of your little life begins.

What discoveries will you make?

What new accomplishment awaits?

What will spark your laughter?

What will bring forth tears?

Each day is a new adventure for you and those who love you.

And each day is a precious gift, of immeasurable value for its uniqueness.

Faces of Love

So fragile and new...So innocent and sweet...

Such gentle breathing...Such tiny fingers curled into little fists...

You sleep so peacefully,

Oblivious to the fact that you are indeed a miracle,

And you so graciously let me stare.

When you awaken—now and always—

may you look up and see faces of love inexpressible.

The most powerful combination of emotions in the world is not called out by

any cosmic event, nor is it found in novels or history books; merely, it is found

by a parent gazing down upon a sleeping child.

ANONYMOUS

The Wonder and Sparkle

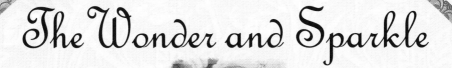

You pull up on your cradle now, fascinated by all there is to see in the world of your bedroom and delighting in the loving company of your sisters. I watch and cherish these moments, discovering anew—with you to guide me—the wonder that lies in the ordinary, the sparkle hidden in the everyday and savoring with each step of our journey together the wonder that you are and the sparkle that you add to my life.

There are many things I admire in children, but the one that impresses me the most is the way they can get the thrill of a lifetime out of the little things that we adults usually can't be bothered with.

O.A. BATTISTA

Your Innocent World

I caught you in a moment of play. And, oh, how this quick glimpse into your innocent world refreshes and renews. You live in the moment—its magic and its fun. Whatever the avenue—kittens and dolls, puppies and trucks—you savor the present. You wholeheartedly delight in the moment as if you are somehow aware that it is all we have. And, thankfully, my child, your approach to this adventure called life is wonderfully contagious! How you make me smile!

A child's life has no dates, it is free,
silent, dateless. A child's life ought to be
a child's life, full of simplicity.

OSWALD CHAMBERS

The Chapters In Your Life

Where will you travel, my child? Today we travel together through the pages of this book. But soon you'll travel alone. You'll journey through your own books...and your own travels will take you away as the chapters in your life are written. But for now I travel with you, delighting in the pages as they unfold and in the questions and wonderings they prompt.

If a child is to keep alive his inborn sense of wonder, he needs the companionship of at least one adult who can share it, rediscovering with him the joy, excitement and mystery of the world we live in.

RACHEL CARSON

Marvel and Delight

Did that butterfly catch your eye as you rode off to places unknown? You noticed that little creature and stopped your journey of imagination to stare. That simple, unthinking action speaks of your ongoing fascination with a world which does indeed call us to marvel and wonder and delight in it. May you never stop noticing the butterflies, my little one.

God sends children for another purpose than merely to keep up the race—to enlarge our hearts; and to make us unselfish and full of kindly sympathies and affections; to give our souls higher aims; to call out all our faculties to extended enterprise and exertion; and to bring round our firesides bright faces, happy smiles, and tender, loving hearts. My soul blesses the great Father every day, that He has gladdened the earth with little children.

MARY HOWITT

Sandra Kuck

Every Wonderful Moment

"If only I could freeze this moment..." That's a thought I've had since the minute you were born. But any moment I'd choose would cost me so many others with you. As I've watched you grow, every wonderful moment and age and stage has given way to another moment and age and stage wonderful in a different way. Each step has its unique demands and its once-in-a-lifetime joys. And each step is priceless as I discover who you are and rediscover the world through your eyes and your heart.

What Is a Girl?

Little girls are the nicest things that happen to people. They are born with

a little bit of angelshine about them and though it wears thin sometimes, there is always

enough left to lasso your heart—even when they are sitting in the mud, or crying

temperamental tears, or parading up the street in mother's best clothes.

A little girl can be sweeter (and badder) oftener than anyone else in the world. She can jitter

around, and stomp, and make funny noises that frazzle your nerves; yet just when

you open your mouth, she stands there demure with that special look in her eyes.

A girl is Innocence playing in the mud, Beauty standing on its head,

and Motherhood dragging a doll by the foot.

ALAN BECK

What Is a Boy?

Between the innocence of babyhood and the dignity of manhood we find a delightful creature called a boy. Boys come in assorted sizes, weights, and colors, but all boys have the same creed: to enjoy every second of every minute of every hour of every day and to protest with noise (their only weapon) when their last minute is finished and the adult males pack them off to bed at night.

Boys are found everywhere—on top of, underneath, inside of, climbing on, swinging from, running around, or jumping to. Mothers love them, little girls hate them, older sisters and brothers tolerate them, adults ignore them, and Heaven protects them. A boy is Truth with dirt on its face, Beauty with a cut on its finger, Wisdom with bubble gum in its hair, and the Hope of the future with a frog in its pocket.

ALAN BECK

The Season for Children

It's the season of gifts...of surprises...of joy. No wonder it's the season for children. For you, my child, are indeed a precious gift...a delightful surprise each new day...and an endless source of joy for me. Of all the gifts I've received, you are the one I treasure most.

Children are a gift of the Lord.

THE BOOK OF PSALMS

A Touch of Grace

This moment is a touch of grace, Little One. So rarely do you sit still these days! You have tea parties to attend to, dollies to care for, flowers to gather, and songs to sing. So I don't take for granted this sweet chance to be quiet with you, to notice your soft skin and gentle breathing and—even after all these years—to savor the wonder of your presence. I cherish this fleeting and precious opportunity to hear about what's going on in that sensitive little heart...to learn what your busy little mind is processing...to dream with you...

May every one of those dreams come true.

Our children are here to stay, but our babies and toddlers and preschoolers are gone as fast as they can grow up—and we have only a short moment with each. When you see a grandfather take a baby in his arms, you see that the moment hasn't always been long enough.

ST. CLAIR ADAMS SULLIVAN

The Joy of You

You're a picture as you sit there. I can't stare hard enough or long enough at your golden curls and bright eyes. So once again—as I've done so many times since your birth—I try to etch into my mind this image from your childhood. Only yesterday you were a tiny thing, and I marveled at your tiny fingers and tiny toes, your delicate ears and sweet little nose. Now you're walking and talking, laughing and singing. You bring joy in different ways today, not the least of which is the joy of simply looking at you. Do you have any idea how precious you are?

What feeling is so nice as a child's hand in yours? So small, so soft and warm, like a kitten huddling in the shelter of your clasp.

MARJORIE HOLMES

Appalachian Lullabye

Well I love my baby
Sweet and fair
You've got the sky in
  your eyes
The sun in your hair
I rock you to sleep most
  every night
And sing you this song
While I hold you tight

Sleep my baby
The angels keep you from
  harm
And your Father above
Cradles you in his love
Safe and warm

Sleep my baby
Nestled in your mama's
  arms
Sleep my baby
  The angels keep you
  from harm

My baby
You'll be sleepin' soon
Kissed by the golden stars
  and moon
I have just one wish for you
May your every dream
  come true

TANYA GOODMAN &
MICHAEL SYKES